BLUE HEAT

Other books by the author

JesusDevil: The Parables

Yabo

Warrior Poet, An Autobiography of Audre Lorde

An Enchanted Hair Tale

Don't Explain: A Song of Billie Holiday

Na Ni

Spirits in the Streets

BLUE HEAT
ALEXIS DE VEAUX

A Sapphic Classic from
Sinister Wisdom

Sinister Wisdom, Inc.
2333 McIntosh Road
Dover, FL 33527
sinisterwisdom@gmail.com
www.sinisterwisdom.org

Designed by Nieves Guerra.
Transcription by Kesso Abduladze.
Copyedit and review by Ivy Marie.

First edition, July 2024

Sinister Wisdom 133
Summer 2024

ISBN-13: 978-1-944981-72-3

Printed in the U.S. on recycled paper.

Contents

ELECTRIFIED MAGNETS

this book is for the life in writing

Forty years ago, Alexis DeVeaux published a portfolio of typewritten poems and hand-drawn illustrations. "This book is for independent publishing," she wrote on the dedication page. DeVeaux's words and artwork had already come into the world multiple times in books by major publishers. So why make blue folders? Why print shocks of hair in even bluer ink? Why invent something she called *Diva Enterprises* when she was already a recognized published author?

This was the gist of one of the first questions I asked the great Alexis DeVeaux when I interviewed her via phone for my dissertation in 2007. Alexis explained (to Alexis) that in the mid-1980's mainstream publishing's attempts to co-opt a Black arts aesthetic had run its course. Revolutionary Black women writers had had their decade and now it was back to striving. Now it was back to desperate upward mobility. Or publishing between the lines. A novel. A collection of short stories maybe. Inclusion meant staying in the boxes. But not for Alexis.

"I will make my own books if publishers don't want my own books and I will sell them in my house, I will sell them on streetcorners," she said.

And indeed, Alexis had tested the power of working out of her own home. Throughout the 1970s she and Gwendolen Hardwick had used their Brooklyn apartment as a space for Flamboyant Ladies literary salons, transforming their residence into a performance space, a social hub, and a place for thinking through the implications of foreign policy, nuclear energy and more. In her living room, Alexis had convened "The Gaptooth Girlfriends"—a writing workshop that included emerging writers like Jewelle Gomez, Irma Gonzalez and more. Each cohort created their own press to publish anthologies of their writing from the workshop. *Gaptooth Girlfriends: The Third Act,* for example, was published by "Third Act Press," the same year Alexis published *Blue Heat.*

Alexis's assessment that times had changed and that publishing was returning to a more repressive mode post 1970s was well-informed. From the late 1970s into the early 1980s she had been working at *Essence Magazine* as poetry editor and editor-at-large. From 1979 to 1984, she and her dear friend Cheryll Y. Greene were able to make good on their mission to bring a transnational Black feminist ethic to the women reading and talking about *Essence* at the beautyshop. They proposed, edited and published pieces by their friend June Jordan about Black women in Nicaragua, De Veaux's own work about solidarity with Haitian migrants and southern African revolutionaries and more. But by 1984, the year before De Veaux self-published *Blue Heat*, the boot came down.

Specifically, the featured image in the article "Inside Grenada" by Jean Wiley about the US invasion of Grenada, which showed the boot of an American soldier stomping on a skinny Grenadian youth got too much attention and brought complaints from the mainstream

US corporations who felt the need to remind the advertising department at *Essence* that they were the real clients of *Essence*, funding the magazine to access the substantial buying power of Black households through the attention of Black women. And so the direct culpability of the US in violently ending a socialist revolution in the Caribbean, told from the perspective of a Black woman who had travelled to Grenada in solidarity with the revolutionaries would not do.

It was in a conversation published in *Essence* though that Alexis DeVeaux theorized exactly the approach to autonomy that gave her the audacity to publish *Blue Heat* in whatever form she chose. In her 1981 conversation with the poet June Jordan whom Alexis calls "sovereign," when she declares that "poems are housework" the two poets articulate a planetary politics of the place you are making.[1] A domestic relationship to the possibility of a liveable earth. And indeed June Jordan's most explicitly anti-imperialist vision emerges in her book of poems entitled what? *Living Room*.

And so if *Blue Heat* only reached the people who came into Alexis's living room it was worth printing. Because as US publishing buckled to a conservative backlash, the AIDS crisis emerged making the need for a revolutionary Black feminist poetics of practice even more urgent.

"We lost so many artists of color during that period of the AIDS epidemic. I lost so many friends. It was about making a decision to be alive. When you're doing

---

1 "Creating Soul Food" *Essence Magazine* April 1981 p. 82-150

these things, the hindsight is wonderful. When you're in the thick of it you know that you are just trying to stay you."

And so we understand that when in her dedication Alexis De Veaux says that *Blue Heat* is "for the life in writing" she means more than the career of a writer. She means more than the distillation of "writer" as an identity. She is talking about writing as a life-giving technology, as a life-sustaining tool, as a means of survival in the face of death and silencing. She means writing and sharing as a worthwhile challenge and practice even if the pages blow away and the folder fades and everyone who stopped by your living room or saw you on the streetcorner tucked the folder away and lost it.

But that's not what happened. *Blue Heat* survives. It reached me through my mentor Cheryll Y. Greene and became a major focus of my PhD dissertation on *The Queer Survival of Black Feminism*. And now it is reaching you as a testament to Alexis De Veaux's theory of survival which she articulates in her introduction to *Gaptooth Girlfriends: The Third Act*:

"CONTINUITY. The will to survive. Believe in the unseen. Sheer and delicate. Belief in self. In another Black woman. A risky idea. To support it by paying for it. Unite to ignite. To know that we are doing it. Got to do. To be a movement: build it in stages: like a bridge. Be one/a bridge. Change the world. And take our lives and make them better. Thrust them forward."

Yes. Survive. What we Got. To do.

this book is for power and joy and change

So what are the thermodynamics of *Blue Heat?* Blue is the hottest part of the flame. The inner part. The ultra-violet part that theorist Denise Ferreria da Silva calls the impact of Blackness to effect change on a molecular level. *Blue Heat* is in direct kinship with blues technologies as poetics of Black survival. It is about transforming what we have into what we didn't know we needed.

Blue Heat is quantum and non-linear. And as I sit here engaging what seems like the linear task of writing an introduction to the fortieth anniversary re-issue of *Blue Heat* I have to honor the way energy actually works.

Because it is no mere coincidence that Alexis wrote *Blue Heat* forty years ago and now another Alexis is welcoming you into it. The poetics of the very universe is at play in that repetition.

Here is a half-life testament. Twenty years ago I sat, huge hair, giant plastic earrings, and all, in a black t-shirt I acrylic printed with a bar-code and the cost of my ivy league tuition in the brownstone home of the Lesbian Herstory Archives. I was looking through the African Ancestral Lesbian Collection created as an afterlife of a foundational lesbian of color group called the Salsa Soul Sisters. And I found an invitation. "Flamboyant Ladies" it said. And there it was: a hand drawn image, doubled of a woman with so much wild hair, huge earrings (because otherwise how would you see them?), open eyes, pursed lips. She was there twice. I was there reflected. I don't know if she/they blinked because I don't know if

13

I/we blinked. The invitation was to a performance that promised to shift your consciousness. It was almost too much when I read to the bottom and saw that the invitation was *from* Alexis.

Sometimes you have to close the archival folder and take a breath. Sometimes you have to publish the whole folder and take your chances. The deep fertility of heat recognizes everything around it as flammable given enough contact. The flamboyant reality is that we will be touched. We will be changed. We will touch. We will change. And it is the repetitive structure of a blues song, or a glitch repetition in the universe that will show us the erotics of our own survival.

and the sheer naked pleasure of rebellion

The energy of *Blue Heat* and the ultraviolet moment it came out of does not only survive through stationary doppelgangers turned introduction-writers. It burns its own path through Alexis De Veaux's body of work up to today. "The Woman Who Lives in the Botanical Gardens" lives on in *Yabo's* genderqueer time traveling fierceness. "New Body: New Life" lives on in Alexis's caring and transformative depiction of Audre Lorde in the process of surviving with and through cancer. Her work to simultaneously bemoan and embody prophecy in "Are There No More Prophets" lives on in *JesusDevil: The Parables'* nuanced queering of the idea of form and embodiment itself. The totem in the internal drawing entitled "Blue Heat" lives on in the parable "interspecies" in *JesusDevil* and in future work where dog subjectivity queers the idea of the human. The insistence in "Cutting the Pattern of the Dream" for South Africa to rise up or "woza" lives on in the life of the dog Woza that Alexis and her partner Sokari are raising together. And won't you find a precedent for your hairstyle, your bravery, your longing here?

These poems, drawing on an ancestral blues aesthetic resource, would also have to find the echoes in the future Alexis makes possible with her living, her protection of her own audacity, because the poems in this portfolio are ahead of their time. "Praise Song for My Sister Rose" precedes the articulated disability justice movement and sings in chorus with Kamilah Aisha Moon's poetry debut *She Has a Name* which she wrote in honor of her own sister. "Cheese Poem" and the whole "Electrified Magnets" section precede what adrienne maree brown, Alexis's most recent publisher, calls *Pleasure Activism* and what pansexual recording artist Janelle Monae calls "The Age of Pleasure."

Or maybe *Blue Heat* beckoned, calling of this, all of us, into being.

and for how i feel now

Maybe it is the form of the blue folder, but I have always seen *Blue Heat* as an assignment. Its honesty about violence, its geopolitical scale, its intimate bravery. What sears our eyes, fingers, tongues as we read, turn the page, speak the words of this collection is the heat of the work that remains to be done.   And what if each poem is an assignment?   You don't need my guidance to find your own assignment in each poem.   Also, these poems are more than what they will teach you in one reading.   They will teach you again and again.

Alexis Pauline Gumbs
Summer 2024

If A Poem Could. . . Then

This book is for my sister, Rose. And for all my sisters blood and born. For my brothers. And for you, Osrane. It is for to be free. Souvereign: not second-class. This book is for Grammie. And for my friends. This book is for power joy and change. For the thunder of spirits. Sweet and sour. This book is for something radical.

This book is for the nights.

This book is for the life in writing. The years framed in poems from 1979 to 1985. For how I feel now. Living on this planet.

This book is for independent publishing. Is for the women who came before me. And for love. And faith found. For my pretty. And my mean evil.

This book is for the Company of "NO" (1981) at Henry Street Settlement Theatre/ New York City. And for all those poems including "But: who got the wings in Atlanta," and "Madeleine's Dreads" as well as others in this collection.

This book is for this book. And the sheer naked pleasure of rebellion. This book, this book is here: at last.

Alexis De Veaux
Brooklyn, New York
1985

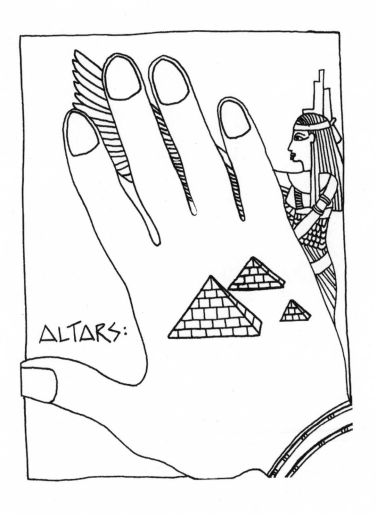

ALTARS:

THE ALTAR OF LIBERATION

Love is one altar.
An altar is a precipice.
A category of experiences.
Invisibility.
Metamorphosis.
Journey.
Pain.
Molting.

A map:
The bones.
So it is.

An altar of liberation:
Libate:
for me.

ROOMS

My mother
manipulated space
what you call
change the house
around
that is, the contents
ever so often
taught me this skill:
try on these rooms
one has got to fit.

PRAISE SONG
FOR MY SISTER ROSE

(September 1, 1945- January 22, 1983)

To learn the meaning of a sister. Daughter
To love her.
To struggle to accept
her.
To be a witness.
To be helpless.

To learn your sacrifices made
possible our victories.
Your polio.
Your shyness.
Being oldest.
15 years at the phone company.

Your friends.
Your lovers.

To remember my rebellion
against you.
As a kid.
As a woman.
To come to know by watching
that you
were not a cripple.

Rose:
these are the things we inherit
from your softness
your worn tennis shoes
neatly placed
one a child's foot
one a woman's foot
stuffed dolls on a closet shelf
17 pennies
clothes that do not fit

Rose: who walked like a woman
and a child
who left us your couragepain
pieces
of your life
we: your family
our mother sisters
brothers cousins
children and kin
we will dance when we think of you
we will sing when we speak of you
and laugh when we see you again
perhaps as a daughter
perhaps as a friend.

A POEM FOR THE DAY OF YOUR WEDDING RECEPTION

(For Mother, and for Donald)

For once:
the graffiti and the subway ride
from Brooklyn to the Bronx
will be festive;
and the newspapers, confetti
to tickle the solitary stares of strangers;

who will beg to come
bearing gifts:
>a thousand shades of evening
>reason to love
>the rustle of sunrise

for once:
we will dance with cowrie shells as teeth
and good luck juju
strung thrice   around our hips
strangers and friends
queens and priestesses
kings;

all of us: Africans.

MADELEINE'S DREADS

Madeleine's dreads
are fertile like the lips
of good friends
intoxicate quick
like an expensive brandy

Madeleine's dreads
are weaved on a loom
of balsam flowers
are planted roots/ exposed
a forest in a fog
unfathomable
are full/ of peppermint oil
olive oil or
vaseline
when everything else
just plain runs out

Madeleine's dreads
are extensions of shake
shake
shekeres
are hand dipped
in mythology & double
dutch tournaments

When Madeleine plays the calebash
she carries OPEC in her hair

she carries the PLO in her hair
she carries the Peoples Republic of Nicaragua
in her hair
on her shoulders

Madeleine's dreads
are full of uprisings in Haiti
and Mississippi
and Brooklyn.

PHYSICAL THERAPY

Take a friday night: and rub
into the skin.

Go out: when the Eye of Horus
appears in the sky.

Expose your heart to the moon.

Expect nothing.

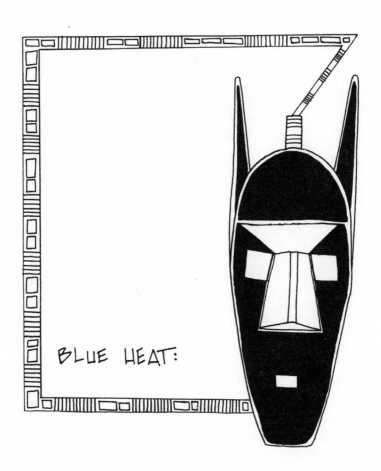

BLUE HEAT:

ARE THERE NO MORE PROPHETS

(For Gwen)

Tonight I will squat in an alleyway of Old
San Juan
and spit out my baby/ feet first
is this the prophet walking away
with no need of nurturing/ not just yet
she is he, and they are God
(I will tell them so when they come)
sure to ask:
are there no more prophets
let the whites flee Africa
and take with them their rhodesias
the ground beneath my city/ feet echoes
with the whistle of bullets popping in Zimbabwe
and the trees in Central Park let down their zippers
and their shameless rain
platters me
I walk by
they do not cover up
I move on

And the scarifications of time
the root of eucalyptus leaves
the fingerprint of pyramids
are woven in a goat path
on the back of my hand

if I never got to Zimbabwe I will still have fought there
if I never get to Zimbabwe I will still have lost my mother
to a refugee camp
but she will say she has moved
from the southbronx to the eastbronx
she has moved from refugee dwelling to refugee status
in the south or east or southwest/ east bronx
refugees outnumber the causes 100 to 1

and the prophets?
are there no more prophets
to see for us/ can we
see/ for ourselves
Africa is the end and the beginning
heaven is the heartbeat
the further down you go
the louder you can hear it/ ask the dead
ask for the resurrection of mythology and love
love, hold me
hold my Africas and prophets
are there no more to say whether or not
it is healthy
to cut off your left arm
because you are right handed
to rape because you are lonely
the problem is still whatcolor/ whichgender
it is not sex
or what sex you sleep with
that is not why/ there are distortions
and no more

prophets in the dank streets
of the bmt
their shrouds fertile with the lice
of elephant shit
as they string together their madnesses/ for beads
one of each color
red for love
pink for success
purple for God/ God
are: there no more to follow the gone
gone divinities
their lives/ a singular sign post
towards the eternal

CHEESE POEM

Good Lord: the government is giving something away.
The government is giving us
high blood pressure and processed cheese:
check it out
line up at your community center
church school or favorite bar
nevermind some whole wheat bread
new shoes
vegetables from the backyard
a lover who spends the night
nevermind
what you want.

"WARNING:
THIS CHEESE HAS A HIGH SALT CONTENT"

nevermind whats underneath the mildew: is that
some more tax breaks for you rich
ketch-up for us poor

so I'm ungrateful:
so its free
so is cancer
so is cold war.
CAUTION: THIS CHEESE IS DANGEROUS
                         TO YOUR HEALTH

the government has some nerve
giving it away
who needs it.

I need some: resurrect the cities: outlaw the Klan
some j-o-b
some a your tongue
poems over breakfast
apple on your breath.

I want something real to go with
something else besides
this dry ass cheese.

IN ANY LANGUAGE,
BREAD WITH DIGNITY

(For Vivian)

She brings fresh brown bread
round and feminine
she says, " you gotta learn
how
to accept help
from your friends,
sweetie "

learn to lean
say what you need
its no shame

granted:
you have to work
at friendship
like you do any community
or garden
got to break through top soil
to whats underneath
plow and plant
get it: under your fingernails
in any language
its fundamental and
global

how many hands does it take
to fertilize a friend
how do I say bread
in my native African
or which part of Africa   I am from

which part of the ingredients
is my face
tears
your wild soft beauty

teach me in Spanish
as we pour tea
and slice bread
and butter it with headlines
and 7 million starve
in Ethiopia
in Haiti: there are food riots
in Harlem: there are breadlines
in prison: there is bread and water

or say it another way:
in Guatemala: there are the disappeared
disposable as breadcrumbs

in any language
you keep the faith
so delicate
behind your glasses

I: am a hungry nation
addicted to bread
my economy
supported by friends
this is what I need
water
flour
salt of sweat
dough
baked with dignity.

CUTTING THE PATTERN
OF THIS DREAM

(For Fatima Dike, South African Poet and Playwright)

I hear it:
the freedom roar
thunderous
hearts and feet
hundreds and hundreds
another generation
lightning electric
cutting the pattern
of this dream
through the nightmare
banished detained uprooted
apartheid

woza
woza South Africa
rise up

and you, my cousin-sister
back home again
with your boot dance
voice
you return
to the tear gas homelands Afrikaneer
evil

to the A.N.C.
and the imagination
of defiance

give me your dreams
across this ocean
I raise my fist
for your Sharpeville breath
for your Soweto fever

give me your hand
and lets become
a human barricade.

BUT:
WHO GOT THE WINGS IN ATLANTA

> I got wings you got wings all Gods
> children got wings when we get
> to heaven   gonna try on our wings
> and fly all over Gods heaven

but:
who got the wings of
who got the hair of
who got the sex
who got the Black
who got the lips of

>> Edward Hope Smith, 14 years old, dead
>> Alfred James Evans, 14 years old, dead
>> Yosef Bell, 9 years old, dead
>> Milton Harvey, 14 years old, dead
>> Angel Lanier, 12 years old, dead

"Angel Lanier was 12 years old at the time of abduction on March 4, 1980. She was a very intelligent young lady who was on the waiting list for the highly touted Montessori School. Her mother, Venus Taylor, said Angel was on her way to visit a friend who lived up the road from her southwest Atlanta home. This is something she did every evening.

According to the Fulton County Public Safety Department, Angel was last seen at her home on March 4th.

According to Ms. Taylor, Angel was last seen by a classmate in a state of shock and delirium on March 7th at the Big Star Supermarket on Cambelton Road, southwest Atlanta. She obviously had gotten away from her abductor for a period of time before her death. Angel Lanier's body was found on March 10, 1980. The coroner's report said she had been strangled to death. She had also been sexually assaulted."

> I got shoes you got shoes all Gods
> children got shoes when we get
> to heaven   gonna put on our shoes
> and walk all over Gods heaven

who
who
who got the nails fingers dreams
scratched knees
bumped head
leap frog
cackle of

> Eric Middlebrooks 14 years old, dead
> Christopher Richardson, 11 years old, dead
> Aaron Wyche, 11 years old, dead
> Anthony B. Carter, 9 years old, dead
> Earl Lee Terrell, 10 years old, dead
> Clifford Jones, 13 years old, dead
> LaTonya Wilson, 7 years old, dead

what if:
what if:
its the Klan
a religious cult/ a cracker
a crazed mothafucka
a Black woman
a Black man

"LaTonya Wilson. . .7 years old. . .was reported missing on Sunday June 22, 1980. She was supposedly taken from her home between the hours of 2am and 6:30am that morning. Her body was found on October 18, 1980 on Atlanta's northwest side. . .That a child can be removed from her home by someone who doesn't know her without other family members or neighbors in adjoining apartments being awakened by noises or screams is beyond me."

beyond me
who
who
got the wings
got the marbles and the dolls
got the tears dirty ears
breath
heart
blood
hunger of
      Aaron Jackson Jr, 9 years old, dead

Patrick Rogers, 16 years old, dead
Charles Stevens, 12 years old, dead
Jeffrey Lamar Mathis, 10 years old, dead
Darron Glass, 10 years old, dead
Lubie "Chuck" Jeter, 14 years old, dead

. . .AND THEN SHE SAID

(For Sara)

question authority
question:
why should trees or rivers or even
stars
be mega-bombed out of orbit

why should you: or me
or my neighbors across the alley
or the kittens
or the flatbush avenue
traffic
disintegrate

why should children
explode

answer:
the government lies.
these are government words:

acceptable casualties
pre-emptive strike
civil defense
limited nuclear war
survivors
what to do (if)

"come to the rally" I urge my mother "if theres a nuclear war, Black or White, we'll all be killed."

"and that aint the half of it" she says "if you open your mouth to one a these teenagers on the bus smoking that shit, you liable to end up with a knife in your guts baby. no respect for your life or nobody elses. as far as people today care."

"think about this" I say.   "we can blow up the world."

"uh huh. you want something to eat?"

the government lies to the people.
this is too painful to believe.
tomorrow may never come.

question authority.

what kind of fuckin world
are we livin in

THE WOMAN WHO LIVES
IN THE BOTANICAL GARDENS

is a man. who. sleeping on a hill
and a bench among the Chinese
maple trees lives there. sleeping in her petticoats
of ackee leaf
and banana leaf though neither grows
in this city: O see: how
tall she is the tallest lean: O see:
the delicate spread of her branch
a thickly muscled arm. how it sways there (quiet)
how it dreams
of plantain and rice and the Black Star Line:
O Jah
and the hairless face/ the primitive hollow of
cheeks taut: with re
bellion. black with the dust of upturned earth and
the plantings of
memory.
O Jah see
O Jah
see: the barest of back/ like an island
and the hair the long: dangling
mats of hair under arm pits: the perfumed hair
laden with anarchy:
hangs from the pit of the arm dangling over the bench.

THE WOMAN WHO LIVES IN THE BOTANICAL GARDENS

wears underneath her
banana ackee leaf petticoat the pants of 3
generations: her grand
father's her father's: her own.
THE WOMAN WHO never comes outside
the gates never comes outside the rags
around her pine bark hair;
the reams of rage: O see, O Jah:

THE WOMAN WHO LIVES IN THE BOTANICAL GARDENS/
THE WOMAN WHO LIVES
IN THE BOTANICAL GARDENS:

is named South Africa.

See there how she
holds the m-16: how she holds the Gardens hostage.
and the bullets
in her earlobes: bullets at her breasts:
the red green and gold
rage. And the necklace of fallopian tube
and the egg of children
and the bits of blood of hair
in the tumours of the homeland: O
Jah: O Jah: see her how she: stalks the gates.
O Jah/ THE WOMAN WHO
THE WOMAN WHO LIVES:
on the squirrels and stray cats of the Garden

LIVES. like a guard dog. gums bared.
teeth pointed: she snap at the gate:

THERE WILL BE NO   VISITORS
AT THE GARDEN TODAY
OR TOMORROW NEITHER
IN FACT
DON'T COME NO CLOSER:
I REALLY DO MEAN TO SHOOT UP
                    THE MUSEUM
I REALLY DO MEAN TO SHOOT UP
                    THE PARKWAY
I REALLY DO MEAN TO SHOOT
                    UP THE HELICOPTER
SO: DON'T COME NO CLOSER

WHO IS ME??
THIS IS SOUTH AFRICA SPEAKING
BLACK SOUTH AFRICA
AND I AM TALKING OVAH THIS SHIT
I: AM TAKING OVAH.

DONT PANIC I SAID

just because ronald reagan won
just because the congress is republican
because they may overturn brown vs the board of ed
because they may revoke the voter registration act
just because theyre weak
just because theyre stupid
dont panic:

jog
run
ride your bike/   consider a gun
do the rope
do the barbells
be firm
be fast
be ready
when they come.

EVERYONE IS NICARAGUA

(For Mercedes, of Esteli/ AMNLAE)

Everyone is a poet there
everyone is the breasted mountains
everyone is the flirting cows
the volcano cerro negro
the cornfields
a stream to bathe in
cafe con leche
everyone is under siege.

Everyone is rice and red beans
everyone is the thick milky night
everyone is the bales of cotton
the sweet watermelon
the eyes of women:
everyone is the scars of Somoza.

Their language makes it so.

"Todas las armas al pueblo"
all arms to the people: si
see how it is in Nicaragua
see how it is in Nicaragua
dust clings tight: new
as the skin of literacy
near the border in Santa Maria

this is what the revolution means:
we have learned to read and write
we know the abc's now
we know the cia.

Everyone is the exploded ports
everyone is the mined harbors
everyone is the thousands dead
the thousands violated
the FSLN graffiti.

Everyone is a poet here
its in the tongue
"siempre un poquito mas. . . el arte arma del pueblo."

Everyone is the spirit of SANDINO
its in the language:
solidaridad
mujere
la cultura
everyone is:
"canto, amour y lucha"
music, love and struggle.

IF THEY COME FOR YOU

(For the New York 8+)

they came
in the morning of night
shadows
silent
viper rattlers
slithering
through: ManhattanQueensBrooklyn
breath of cowardice

they came
500 and more
NYPD FBI
hunted your dreams
slave catchers
deliberate as poison
raided
handcuffed
arrested
your warrior love
for conspiring to conspire
they said
they came
with no evidence
sure as jail
if they come for you

in the morning
they will come for us
that night.

ONE LETTER ALPHABET SONG

A: my name is Africa
there hasnt been much
rain fall   in twen   ty two countries
in ovah a decade
the desert   is
ad   van   cing
and we
are star
v   i   n   g

MODERN DAY LIVING IS HARD ON BLACK WOMEN

"I'll work long as I can then I'll stop"
my Grandmother predicted. At 84 she retired:
a church woman
a maid
a little bonus
bad feet.
"Call me once a week dont forget" she says "I'm alone here.
You never know what will happen. Or how fast."
You never know a Black woman
the guttural
insistent
ache of her.
My Grandmother went back to work.

This is the deal:
modern day living
is hard on a Black woman
it fucks with your frequencies:
You could be coming from a meeting
You could be wanting to help a dude get straight
You could be in the vestibule of your apartment building
You could be sleep Sunday morning in your mommas house
in Philly
some teenage boys come in rape you
rape your momma house
they Black you be Black

You could be glad your 2 daughters aint with you
You could be done wrote books but who cares
you know
You could be dont know nothin bout no word
                                    processor shit
no computers neitha
You could be expecting your check
phone bill overdue
You could be got to fight off
White man and the Black man too

You could be 15
You could be 15 on a school day
You could be sitting in a grown mans lap
in the morning in the park
You could be feel his thing press your butt
You could be sleeping in Penn Station
You could be wanting some love: syncopated
as sucking: want it to swallow you
in a juice of surprise
You could be need your mother
You could be aint talking to her
You could be aint talking to your best friend
You could be need some good sex regular
You could be got too many dependents
You could be cant go to the hospital
who gonna pay for it
You could be dont want to die
You could be dont want to live
You could be killed that baby for crying

You could be killed that baby for crying so much
You could be time to grab somebodys hand
You could be better get a hold of yourself.

ELECTRIFIED MAGNETS:

CUNTERY:

I will make a savannah of my
dreads

I will make an incense of my
pussy

I will make breadfruit of my
hands

I will make a fetish for your
love.

TRAVEL BUG

yeah baby, she say
good thing you aint my woman
you suffer from wander-lust
you aint nevah home
dont answer your phone neitha
not that I was lookin for ya
not that I wantcha
whatsamatter, somebody throw wander
dust round ya door?

DEATH OF AN IDOL

The riot of your laughter
breaks a sound barrier
and what flies up
must certainly
fly down

even the best chinaware
will chip
once
we said of the other
what a good good friend
and overlooked
the cracks
so busy laughing
so busy
busy
and fixed our splintered crystals
with glue
in public
in private
the truth is
we all trespass
without meaning
to
know your bottom line
then draw it
every love

has its fine clauses
and it dont pay
to speed read

LA LUNA DE MI CORAZON

la luna de mi corazon
orbits
from a distance
in planetary desguise
she wears the night
beaded
on her hips,
seduces
then chastises me:
shes afraid
of her light.

TWILIGHT

it is never a come-suddenly:

abrupt as dawn. tearing the darkness or first
light. illumination. erupting sleep
just below the skin of it.

never as visible
as skyline. as the woman on the bridge; nightly. electric.
lapis. not like her tai chi. her pose of black jackal, serene
against city blue/ gray fog: lights.

here: take it, my friend
take this surrealian-blue
mauve
cape of dusk.
the last before we embrace. a tongue behind the knee; to suck
on the she-sex of evening. take some, but take it
easy.

CAMP-ITIS:

Up here in the woods
a quarter moon tongue
kisses my dreams
with sweet saliva

reminds me:

this quiet is ever so
natural
like the shades of your voice
spider webs
the elbow of a tree.

I miss home.

And at night
a lake of stars
above the birch and pine
fondle me
and whisper

        be patient
        be generous with love.

And the absolutely still
water
and fresh cut grass
punctuated by deer droppings

and coyote
who never heard of New York City.

Its strange and cozy here
there is reason
to be myself
I'm thinking:
how do I measure the infinitesimal
and yes, its a damn good camp.

COMPLICATIONS OF THE HEART

Its like this:
we take turns
mold each other into shapely
dresses
progressive as our politics
we know this dance well
even so
we make up the steps
there are no rules
except:
you can tell a diva
by her proximity to the mirror
even so
its complicated
and uncomfortable
out here
where I wait
without social etiquette
dizzy as sentimental
for that second chance
or the pleasure to
slow dance
the last dance
and the first
and its all very polite
but
one of us always has another

lover who cuts in
and we stretch our arms
to welcome
each new dancer
and jealous, I'm told
has no place
in revolutionary love
so really
I cant say what
it is I'm complaining about
but like all free women
I do get the blues.

HANGIN TUFF:

(For Loyce)

when the going gets tough: the tuff turn pro
when the going gets tough: when the going gets
down to a dime I fight sleep and fast: I want the impossible:
revolution in America
the end of world tyranny
a perfect lover.

right now be a good time to come: knock
with your sooty laughter: solid: black as
the fever of freedom
I want you.

and what is the relationship between creativity
and war
and yes baby these are distant proximities
between us: what goes around comes around.

familiar: heat: magnetic
touch me in that firm soft
thighs spread in flight
chisel at the ache: say you
want me
too much too lonely too
bitchy
bitch.

vocabulary frequently used by Black women:
fibroids
welfare   cancer
shitmothafucka
my kids.

women born under the number 6
often suffer with their breasts: in childbirth
are prone to milk fever: months to guard against
for ill-health and overwork: May October November
vital statistics:
70% of Black women harbor fibroid tumors
47% of Black womens children are functionally illiterate.

hang tuff when the going gets rough
hang tuff:
lap around the park
race the pigeons joggers
the nightmares still clinging
shed the skins of dreams
I pump my legs into bigger weapons:
bazookas: bombers: AK47s
swift as survival
try and catch me
the lean mean blue machine
and in the city its all about
camouflage living:
I love you you love her she loves them
tough tittie:

I am not tough:
I want to be soft: hungry: wet

e dough say la la
e nome c da
may na na   haha hume
ha haha   hume

when the going gets tough: the tuff
slice a carrot
chop potato
boil the water:
make soup.

NEW BODY: NEW LIFE:

Alone and shy my finger
navigates
a fuzz of pubic hair
shaven
where the surgeon
split through
alleys of uterus

navigates just above
to a landscape of stitches
"a bikini cut" my doctor
assures me
we admire the map
of his handiwork
"you wont even see it
when the hair grows back."

what will I see
with these new eyes
and this topography
of healing
this tributary
of female problems
from me
to my sister
to my Grandmother
a bloodline
common as transfusion

it is a labor of love
to love yourself

"want to see my incision?"
I ask friends
and compare womb-stories
and the numbness
beneath hospital gowns

the fear
what it takes
to walk and breathe now

look at it kiss it
gently please
this is my scarification
life's beauty mark
to seduce you with.

Accompaniment: Guiding Exercises from Alexis Pauline Gumbs

If you want some accompaniment, here are some guiding exercises as you move through Blue Heat (as Blue Heat moves through you).

IF A POEM COULD...THEN

What is at stake in your practice of reading *Blue Heat*? Remember "this book is for power joy and change." Start by dedicating your practice to a loved one. They may be living, ancestral, older than you or younger than you and of any species. Who is it?

And now dedicate your practice to a miracle involving them that speaks to the way you feel right now.

And then make a declaration based on this dedication miracle:

I am reading Blue Heat as if

_____depends on it.

(e.g. ...as if the possibility of a more honest relationship with my mother depends on it. As if the possibility of my grandmother, an ancestor, releasing all her burdens and elevating depends on it. As if the divine messages that will come from honoring my mentor depend on it. As if my guidance to create a relationship to myself that offers a liberated path to my nieces depends on it.)

ALTARS

Look at your hands. Where are you now? Where have you been? Where are you going? Where have you seen these hands before?

"The Altar of Liberation"
Fill in the blanks:
My altar is on the edge of _____ and
_____.
I water it with _____.
(Repeat 7x)

"Room"
Fill in the Blanks:
The room I am wearing is _____.
I want to empty it of _____.
I want to fill it with _____.

"Praise Song for My Sister Rose"
How do you learn "the meaning of a sister?"

How did you learn the meaning of "daughter?"

"A Poem for the Day of Your Wedding Reception"
Remember a ceremony that may have never happened in your lifetime. Write a blessing towards a ceremony connecting any two people you want to connect and bless.

"Madeleine's Dreads"
Zoom in very closely to an aspect of someone you love.
Imagine the world you would see if that aspect of them
was big enough to live inside. Or you were small enough
to live there.

"Physical Therapy"
Write three expectations that weighed on you this week.
Cross them out.

BLUE HEAT
"Are There No More Prophets"
What will you tell them when they come?

"Cheese Poem"
What you want:

What you need:

What you notice:

"In Any Language, Bread with Dignity"
What is a form of love I think the world needs urgently?

How am I doing at accepting that form of love in my own life?

"Cutting the Pattern of the Dream"
Fill in the blanks:
"give me your dreams
across this _____.
across this _____.
across this _____.
across this _____.
across this _____.
across this _____.
across this _____.

"But: who got the wings in Atlanta"
Just read the names. Hold the names.
Just read the nouns Alexis offers. Hold the nouns.

"…and then she said"
Remember a conversation that has impacted you recently. Why was it important?

"The Woman Who Lives in the Botanical Gardens"
Can you imagine a community you are in solidarity with far away embodied by a person in your local community?

"Everyone is Nicaragua"
Everyone is _____
Everyone is _____
Everyone is _____
Everyone is _____
Everyone is _____
Everyone is _____
Everyone is _____

"If They Come for You"
Who are they?

Who is you?

Who are you in relation to 'they' and 'you'?

"One Letter Alphabet Song"
Choose a letter of the alphabet and move the through the day noticing the poem focusing on that letter offers you.

"Modern Day Living is Hard on Black Women"
What if it is time to grab somebody´s hand? Whose hand? How will you reach out?

What do you notice about how it feels to think about those questions?

ELECTRIFIED MAGNETS
"Cuntery"
There is someone you can thank right now for something they made in honor of you, sensual, romantic or otherwise recently or long ago.

Thank you for _____.
Thank you for _____.
Thank you for _____.
Thank you for _____.
Thank you for _____.
Thank you for _____.
Thank you for your love.

"Travel Bug"
What true thing do they say to you, joking?

"Death of an Idol"
What is a time that you trespassed? What did you learn/ are you learning from that?

"La Luna de Mi Corazon"
What would you do tonight if you weren't afraid of your light?

"Twilight"
Just see if you can notice it today, the twilight.
What did you notice?/Not notice?

"Camp-It is"
What is the last truth nature whispered to you? Where
were you? How is that truth showing up in your life?

"Complications of the Heart"
Describe one of your relationships, maybe the one with
the person you dedicated to, as a dance. What do you
notice or learn?

"Hangin Tuff"
What is the relationship between creativity and war in
your life?

"New Body: New Life"
Write a love poem to one of your scars.

Blue Heat was first published in 1985 by

DIVA PUBLISHING ASSOCIATES
135 Eastern Parkway- Suite 8K
Brooklyn   New York 11238

The following poems were previously published:

"MADELEINE'S DREADS," Open Places, Fall 1982.
"ALTAR OF LIBERATION," and "CHEESE POEM,"
     Ikon Magazine, Summer/Fall 1983, Second Series
     Number 2.

"THE WOMAN WHO LIVES IN THE BOTANICAL
     GARDENS," Confirmation: An Anthology of
     African American Women, edited by Amina and
     Amiri Baraka, William Morrow, New York:1983.

"...AND THEN SHE SAID," Village Voice, Volume 27,
     Number 24, June 1982.

"EVERYONE IS NICARAGUA," Madre Speaks,
     Volume 1, Number 2, November 1984.

Very Special Thanks To:
Loyce Stewart
Marie Brown
Kathy Engel and the staff of MADRE
Blue Mountain Center, New York
Ragged Edge Press

Photo by Sokari Ekine

Alexis De Veaux, PhD, is one of a stellar list of American writers highlighted by LIT CITY, a public art initiative of banners bearing their names and images in downtown Buffalo, New York, in recognition of the city's renowned literary legacy. Co-Founder of The Center for Poetic Healing, a project of Lyrical Democracies (with Kathy Engel), and of the Flamboyant Ladies Theatre Company (with Gwendolen Hardwick), Alexis De Veaux is a Black queer feminist independent scholar whose work in multiple genres is internationally known. Born and raised in Harlem, New York City, De Veaux is published in five languages-English, Portuguese, Dutch,

Japanese and Serbo-Croatian. Over the past five decades her work has appeared in numerous anthologies and publications, most recently in *Mouths of Rain, An Anthology of Black Lesbian Thought* (ed. Briona Simone Jones, 2021). De Veaux is the author of the memoir *Spirits In The Street* (1973); an award-winning children's book, *Nani* (1973); the biography-in-prose, *Don't Explain, A Song of Billie Holiday* (1980); *Blue Heat: A Portfolio of Poems and Drawings* (1985); the poems, *Spirit Talk* (1997); and *An Enchanted Hair Tale* (1987), a recipient of the 1988 Coretta Scott King Award presented by the American Library Association and the 1991 Lorraine Hansberry Award for Excellence in Children's Literature. Her plays include Circles (1972); The Tapestry (1975); A Season to Unravel (1979); NO (1980); and Elbow Rooms (1986).

De Veaux also authored *Warrior Poet, A Biography of Audre Lorde* (2004). The first biography of the pioneering lesbian poet, *Warrior Poet* won several prestigious awards including the Zora Neale Hurston/Richard Wright Foundation Legacy Award, Nonfiction (2005), the Gustavus Meyers Center for the Study of Bigotry and Human Rights Outstanding Book Award (2004), and the Lambda Literary Foundation Award for Biography (2004). In other media, De Veaux's work appears on several recordings, including the highly-acclaimed album, Sisterfire (Olivia Records, 1985). As an artist and lecturer she has traveled extensively throughout the United States, the Caribbean, Africa, Japan and Europe; and is recognized for her ongoing contributions to a number of community-based organizations.

Alexis De Veaux was a tenured member of the faculty of the University at Buffalo, Buffalo, NY, 1992-2013; teaching, most recently, as Associate Professor of Women's and Gender Studies in the Department of Transnational Studies. Her novel, *Yabo*, was published by Redbone Press (2014) and was awarded the 2015 Lambda Literary Award for Lesbian Fiction. She is co-founder (with Amy Horowitz) of The Enclave Habitat, a network of socially conscious international artists and activists. Her latest work, *JesusDevil, The Parables* was published by AK Press in the spring of 2023.

Further information is available on her author website, alexisdeveaux.com.